MAGNETISM

John Woodruff

Photography by
Chris Fairclough

RSVP
RAINTREE
STECK-VAUGHN
PUBLISHERS
The Steck-Vaughn Company

Austin, Texas

Library of Congress Cataloging-in-Publication Data
Woodruff, John.
Magnetism / John Woodruff.
     p.   cm.—(Science Projects)
     Includes bibliographical references and index.
     Summary: Introduces the basic concept of
     magnetism through simple experiments that
     can be performed at home.
     ISBN 0-8172-4946-X
     1. Magnetism—Juvenile literature.
     2. Magnetism—Experiments—Juvenile literature.
     [1. Sound—Experiments. 2. Experiments.]
     I. Fairclough, Chris, ill. II. Title
     III. Series: Science projects.
     QC753.7.W66   1998
     538'.078—dc21   97-24645

Printed in Italy. Bound in the United States.
1 2 3 4 5 6 7 8 9 0 02 01 00 99 98

Picture acknowledgments
The publishers would like to thank the following for permission to reproduce their pictures **E.T. Archive:** page 22; **Science Photo Library:** pages 6 (Alex Bartel), 20 (Alfred Pasieha), 36 (CERN), 43 (Martin Bond), 44 (Marcello Bertinetti), 45 top (Michael Fisher), 45 bottom (Simon Fraser), cover (Bruce Iverson); **Tony Stone Images:** page 24 (Aurora/Johnny Johnson). **Illustrations:** Stefan Chabluk and Julian Baker (cover and page 43).

CONTENTS

WHAT ARE MAGNETS?

A solid object that has the power to attract iron and some other metals is called a magnet. It does this through its magnetic field, a region of force surrounding it: the more intense the field, the stronger the magnet.

Objects that are attracted to the magnet "feel" a force, called magnetism, when they are inside the magnetic field. This magnetic force can pass through some materials. Even a weak magnet will attract a pin on the other side of a sheet of paper, for example.

magnets and magnets in the form of a disk or a stubby cylinder. Every magnet has two poles, called north and south, at opposite parts of it: at the two ends of a horseshoe magnet, for example, or on the two sides of a disk.

Powerful magnets can be made by passing an electric current through wire coiled around a piece of iron. The result is called an electromagnet. Magnets are used in many household and everyday devices. They are also commonly used in industrial machinery, usually in the form of electromagnets.

Magnets come in several different shapes. A familiar one is the curved horseshoe magnet. There are also bar

MAKE A MODEL THEATER

MATERIALS
- a large shoe box with a lid
- white poster board
- scissors
- masking tape
- glue
- two sticks or dowels about 12 in. (30 cm) in length
- two magnets
- large steel paper clips
- paints or crayons

1. Place the shoe box on its side lengthways on the lid and draw around it. Cut a hole in the lid slightly smaller than the rectangle you have drawn.

2. Cut strips out of the short ends of the lid, about .5 in. (1 cm) from the edge. Glue the shoe box sideways onto its lid.

3. Draw and color the characters of your play on the sheets of poster board. Make sure to allow enough extra to bend backward for the base of your figure. Now cut out each character and tape a paper clip to its base. Tape a strip of poster board to the back and base, so that it stands upright.

4. Securely tape a magnet to the end of each stick.

5. Make a slot in the top of the theater by cutting along the length of the box near the back of the theater. Cut a piece of poster board to fit into the slot. Draw and color your "backdrop" or use pictures cut from magazines. Make as many backdrops as you wish.

6. Insert a backdrop into the slot and place the characters on the stage. Poke the sticks with the taped-on magnets through the spaces cut at the ends of the shoe box lid. Use your sticks to move the characters about the stage.

The theater works because magnetism penetrates the cardboard shoe box, and cardboard is nonmagnetic.

# MAGNETIC MATERIALS

The theater on page five works because magnets attract some materials, like the paper clips on the characters, but not others, like the stage. Scientists divide all substances into magnetic materials—the ones that a magnet will attract—and nonmagnetic materials.

Some metals and alloys are magnetic materials. An alloy is a metal with other ingredients mixed in to make it stronger or rustproof. One of the most common metals is iron. Pure iron is a magnetic material and is used to make magnets. Many everyday objects are made of steel, which is an alloy of iron. Pins, paper clips, and cutlery are often made of steel and will be attracted to a magnet. Special steels make some of the best magnets.

Two other metals, cobalt and nickel, and their alloys are magnetic materials. The oxides of some metals, such as chromium dioxide (chromium combined with oxygen), are also magnetic. Most metals, however, are not magnetic.

Materials that are not metals, for example rubber, are not magnetic. But iron can be mixed with rubber while it is being manufactured to produce a flexible magnetic material, sometimes used for refrigerator magnets.

A huge magnet is used in this scrapyard to separate magnetic materials from nonmagnetic materials. This is an electromagnet, which uses electricity to boost its magnetism. It picks up metal objects, moves them, and lets them go again when the current is turned off.

DID YOU KNOW?

Some metals are repelled by a magnet. Such metals are said to be diamagnetic. Bismuth is an example of a diamagnetic metal.

WHAT IS MAGNETIC?

1. Put together a range of objects to include ones that you think will not be magnetic as well as those you expect might be.

2. Divide the objects into two groups: ones you think are made of a magnetic material, and ones you think are not.

3. Test each object with the magnet, and write down whether it was attracted. Note down also how strongly it was attracted. Were you surprised by anything?

4. Think about how to present your results. Make separate lists for magnetic and nonmagnetic objects or for ones you predicted correctly and ones you got wrong.

5. Get some friends to do the tests with their own selection of objects. Then compare results.

MATERIALS

- a variety of small objects made of different materials
- a strong magnet

ATTRACT OR REPEL?

We usually think of magnets as objects that attract other metals. However, if you experiment with two magnets, you will find that in some positions they attract each other, but that in other positions there is a force that tries to push them apart: they repel each other. These forces of attraction and repulsion come about because every magnet has two poles, called north and south. When you bring two magnets together, they will be repelled if the poles facing each other are the same—both north or both south. If the two poles are the same, they are called "like" poles. When the poles facing each other are different ("unlike" poles), the magnets attract each other.

A magnet's poles have been known as north and south ever since magnetic compasses were first used for navigation (see page 22). The pole of the compass's magnetic needle that pointed north was called the "north pole"—a shortening of "north-seeking pole." It is, of course, the needle's south pole that points north, because unlike poles attract, but the name has stuck.

You can test whether a small metal object is magnetic by bringing a magnet up to it. If the object is attracted when the magnet is one way around but repelled when the magnet is turned the other way, then you know that the object itself is a magnet.

TESTING FOR POLES

1. Make a frame by nailing the 12-in. (30-cm) length of wood to the baseboard and the 6-in. (15-cm) length to the top of the 12-in. piece.

2. Loop the thread around both ends of the bar magnet and use adhesive tape to secure the loops around the horizontal part of the frame. The magnet should be level.

3. Bring the other magnet alongside it so that two poles are close together. What happens?

4. Repeat step **2**, trying all combinations of north and south poles to confirm which repel and which attract.

MATERIALS

- two identical strong bar magnets with north and south poles marked
- strong thread
- a piece of wood 12 in. x 4 in. (30 cm x 10 cm) for the baseboard
- two pieces of .75-in. (2-cm) square wood, one 12-in. (30-cm) long and one 6-in. (15-cm) long
- a hammer & thin nails
- masking tape

MAGNETIC LEVITATION

1. Place one of the bar magnets at the center of the Styrofoam base and draw around the magnet with a pencil.

2. Push a toothpick firmly into each end of your penciled rectangle, and along the sides of the rectangle at intervals of about .5 in. (1 cm).

3. When this "fence" is complete, replace the bar magnet.

4. Put the second bar magnet on top of the first so that the two north poles are at the same end. What happens?

MATERIALS

- two identical strong bar magnets with north and south poles marked
- a Styrofoam block
- toothpicks
- a pencil

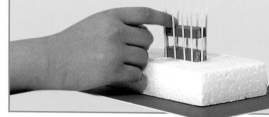

MORE LEVITATION

For this experiment you will need the frame you made for the project on page 8.

1. Tie one end of the thread to the paper clip, and tape the other end to the baseboard.

2. Tape a bar magnet to the horizontal part of the frame. You will find that the paper clip is kept in the air by the attraction of the magnet.

3. If you like, you can decorate the clip by attaching to it a small picture of a bird or aircraft on a thin piece of paper.

MATERIALS

- a strong bar magnet with north and south poles marked
- 12 in. (30 cm) of thread
- a sheet of thin paper
- masking tape
- a small steel paper clip

9

MAGNETIC STRENGTH

Magnets vary in how strongly they will attract magnetic materials. You can tell this by the difference in the pull you feel when you move different magnets up to a magnetic object. The strength of a magnet depends on several things. Bigger magnets are usually, but not always, stronger than smaller ones. A magnet's strength also depends on the substance it is made of, how it was made, and its shape.

A magnet exerts most of its strength through its poles, although the positions of poles vary in differently shaped magnets. Bar magnets and horseshoe magnets pull most strongly at their ends, but disk magnets behave differently. Test them and see!

Powerful magnets can be very useful in industry and research, but sometimes their strength needs to be confined.

MEASURING A MAGNET'S STRENGTH (1)

1. Place the sheet of paper on a flat level surface, and place the ruler on the paper. Tape the ends of the ruler to the paper so that it doesn't move.

2. Put a paper clip next to the ruler, near one end, with its end by a convenient mark on the ruler.

3. Place one of the magnets alongside the ruler, at the other end from the paper clip, and slowly slide it toward the clip until the clip just begins to move.

4. Use the pencil to mark the position of the magnet when this happens, and measure the distance between the clip and the magnet.

5. Repeat steps **3** and **4** a few times. Average your results.

6. Repeat steps **3** to **5**, using different magnets.

7. Which of the magnets was strongest? Rank them in order of strength.

MATERIALS

- various magnets, including two different bar magnets and a horseshoe magnet
- a ruler
- a pencil
- masking tape
- a sheet of glossy white paper
- a steel paper clip

Weak magnets have their uses too. Popular board games such as chess and checkers come in magnetic versions that can be played while traveling. The magnets are just strong enough to hold the pieces on their squares. Some screwdrivers are lightly magnetic—just strong enough to hold a screw while it is maneuvered into an awkward spot.

MEASURING A MAGNET'S STRENGTH (2)

1. Take one of the magnets and attach a paper clip to its end.

2. Attach a second clip to the first one, which will now be acting as a magnet too, and continue to add further clips, building up a chain.

3. When no more can be added, or the chain breaks, note the largest number that could be attached.

4. Repeat steps **1** to **3**, using different magnets. Also, see how many paper clips can be attached to different parts of the magnets.

5. Which of the magnets was strongest? Rank them in order of strength. Did methods 1 and 2 give the same rankings?

MATERIALS
- the same group of magnets that you used in method 1 on the previous page
- steel paper clips (must be all the same)

# MAGNETIC PENETRATION

When you use a magnet to pick up a paper clip, the magnetic force of attraction between the magnet and the clip is acting first of all through air. The air between them does not do much to hinder the magnetic force—in fact, if you could carry out the experiments on the previous pages in a vacuum or in outer space, you would get much the same results.

A magnet can act through a more substantial barrier. As long as the barrier is made of a nonmagnetic material, a magnet will still attract a magnetic material on the other side of the barrier. Refrigerator magnets stick to the door of a refrigerator, but the outer surface of the refrigerator door isn't metal; it is a protective coating covering the metal of the door itself. The magnetic force penetrates the coating and allows the magnet to stay in place. The force will also act through a sheet of paper, so you can use the magnet to hold a shopping list in place on the door.

WHAT WILL MAGNETISM PENETRATE?

1. Take a sheet of a flexible material, like paper, and wrap it around the bar magnet so that just one layer is covering one of the poles. See if you can pick up the paper clip with this end of the magnet. Continue adding more layers, checking as you do so whether you can still pick up the paper clip. How many layers did you add?

2. Now do the same with some of the other materials. With some you may have to cut up the materials to get more layers around the end of the magnet. Record the highest number of layers of each material you used while you were able still pick up the clip.

MATERIALS

- a bar magnet
- a range of different materials such as pieces of paper, thin cardboard, plastic, cloth, and aluminum foil
- containers of different materials, including ones of glass, china, and plastic
- scissors
- plastic wrap
- steel paper clips
- wood blocks or books as supports

3. For more rigid materials, like sheets of plastic, place them between two supports with the paper clip resting on top. Bring the magnet up from underneath and see if you can move the clip. Again, record your results for each material you use.

4. Put one or two paper clips in one of the containers and see if you can remove them by using the magnet from the outside. Repeat this step, using the other containers.

5. Fill one of the containers with water and drop in a paper clip. Protect the magnet carefully with the plastic wrap. Lower the magnet into the water and see how close to the paper clip it needs to be to pick up the clip.

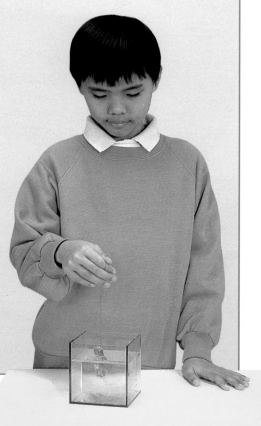

DID YOU KNOW?

Doctors can examine a patient's insides by a technique called magnetic resonance imaging (MRI). The equipment uses a magnet to "reach" into the body and make the atoms in body parts behave like magnets. This makes it possible for images to be recorded, much like X-ray pictures.

Were these fair tests? If you had more equipment, how might you improve them? What do your results for the aluminum foil tell you about the material it is made from?

 # SHIELDING MAGNETS

As we have seen, very powerful magnets are used in industry and research. The more powerful a magnet is, the greater the distance over which its magnetic force will affect magnetic materials. This can cause problems. In a laboratory, a powerful magnet will affect nearby equipment and instruments containing steel parts. Computers and computer disks (see pages 32–33) will be affected too.

The solution is to enclose the magnet and the area where it is being used within a magnetic shield. Because magnetic force will penetrate a non-magnetic material, magnetic shields are made of a material that is magnetic. The field is "trapped" by the material of the shield, and though it passes through the shield, it is much weaker outside.

Magnetic shields can be used to keep magnetism out as well as in. A sensitive piece of equipment being used near a powerful magnet can be enclosed in its own shield to protect its components. Accurate compasses are protected in this way.

Computers and computer disks are affected by powerful magnets. Sensitive equipment can be protected by a magnetic shield, which is inside the computer.

TESTING MAGNETIC SHIELDS

For this experiment you will need the the frame you made for the project on page 8.

1. Tie about 10 in. (25 cm) of thread to the paper clip and tape the other end of the thread to the baseboard.

2. Tape the magnet to the horizontal part of the frame.

3. Pick up the paper clip so that the thread is taut and make the paper clip "fly" (see page 9).

4. Now move the metal lid so that it comes between the magnet and the clip. Don't touch either of them with the lid.

5. From what you notice, do you think the metal lid is acting as a magnetic shield?

6. Try using "shields" made of other materials. What happens?

# MAGNETIC INDUCTION

An object made from a magnetic material can be turned into a magnet that will attract other magnetic objects. The process of making a magnet is called magnetic induction, or magnetization. We have seen how a magnet can pick up a "chain" of paper clips. This is because each added clip becomes a magnet (magnetism is induced in it) and it attracts another clip. But when the clips are removed, they are no longer magnets. They were temporary magnets.

It is also possible to make an object keep its magnetic power when the inducing magnet is taken away. The result is known as a permanent magnet. A magnetic material that can be made permanently magnetic is called ferromagnetic. A simple way of making one is to stroke a magnetic object, such as an iron nail or knitting needle, with a magnet. The stroking must be done in one direction only, like stroking a cat. (This is explained on page 26.)

A permanent magnet can also be made by placing the object inside a coil of wire and passing a current from a battery through the coil (see pages 34–35).

MAKE A TEMPORARY MAGNET

MATERIALS
- a steel screw and an iron nail
- a strong bar magnet
- steel paper clips

1. Place the screw against a bar magnet.

2. Keeping the screw in contact with the magnet, see if it will attract a paper clip.

3. Hold the screw steady and slowly move the magnet away from it. Does the screw keep its magnetism?

4. Repeat steps **1** to **3** with the nail. Is there any difference?

5. Think about how the test could be varied, perhaps by keeping the screw or the nail in contact with the magnet for longer, and repeat. Does anything make a difference?

MAKE A PERMANENT MAGNET

1. Hold the steel nail, and stroke it with the magnet as shown in the photograph opposite. Move the magnet down the length of the nail, lift, and repeat. Always use the same end of the magnet.

2. After 20 strokes, stop and, using the test described on page 7, check to see whether the nail has become magnetized. Measure and record its strength. (You can use one of the tests on pages 10–11.)

3. Give the nail 20 more strokes, making 40 in all, and repeat the strength test.

4. Test the strength after 60 and 80 strokes. Does the magnet's strength increase each time, and by how much?

5. Repeat steps 1 to 4, using an iron nail. Do your results differ?

6. Take a different iron nail, and this time stroke it with two bar magnets together as shown in the diagram. Use a smooth stroking action as before, but start in the middle with the two magnets close together, and move them simultaneously toward opposite ends. Always keep the north pole of one magnet and the south pole of the other toward the nail.

7. After every 20 strokes, test the strength. How do the results compare at each stage with those when you used the nail stroked with just one magnet?

8. How permanent are your permanent magnets? Test the strength of one of them after an hour, a day, and a week.

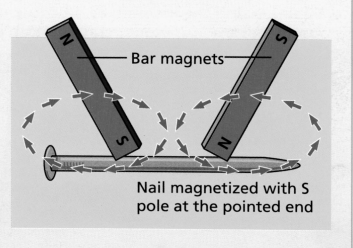

Bar magnets

Nail magnetized with S pole at the pointed end

DEMAGNETIZATION

Just as a piece of iron or steel can be magnetized, a magnet can be demagnetized—made to lose some or all of its magnetic power. Another word for this is degaussing, named after the German scientist Carl Friedrich Gauss, who studied magnetism in the early nineteenth century.

There are several ways in which a magnet can become demagnetized. It can happen if the magnet gets banged: if you hit a magnet with a hammer, or drop it on the floor, it will lose some of its magnetism. If strong magnets are mishandled they will sooner or later become weak. Another way of lessening a magnet's power is to heat it. A third way is to place the magnet in a coil and pass an alternating electric current through it. An alternating current reverses direction many times a second and this disrupts the magnetic power.

Sometimes it is necessary to demagnetize magnetic materials. Television sets and computer monitors use magnetic fields to produce an image on their screens, and it is important that other parts of them not be magnetized. Some computer monitors have a control marked "degauss," while others automatically degauss at startup.

SHAKING

1. Fill the test tube nearly to the top with iron filings, and fit the cork tightly. There should be a small space between the filings and the cork.

2. Magnetize the filings in the tube by stroking it 50 times with the magnet, as described on page 17. Test the tube-magnet's strength by seeing how many paper clips it will pick up.

3. Shake the tube for about three seconds, and test its strength again.

4. Repeat step **3** until there is no further change in the strength. Has all the magnetism disappeared?

MATERIALS
- a test tube with a cork
- iron filings
- a strong bar magnet
- steel paper clips

WARNING!
- Do not demagnetize actual magnets! The bar magnet is used here only to magnetize the iron filings.

STRIKING

1. Test the magnetic strength of the magnetized steel screw by seeing how many paper clips it will pick up.

2. Using the pliers to grip the screw tightly, give it 10 sharp taps with the hammer. (Watch your fingers!) Test its strength again.

3. Repeat step 2 until there is no further change in the strength. Has all the magnetism disappeared?

MATERIALS
- a strong bar magnet
- a steel screw, magnetized as described on page 17
- a hammer
- a pair of pliers

HEATING

1. Holding the screw with the pliers, heat it until it just starts to glow. Leave it somewhere safe (perhaps outside, on a concrete path) for at least 10 minutes to cool down.

2. When it has cooled down, test its magnetic strength.

3. Repeat steps **1** and **2**, taking care to heat the screw for the same length of time in each case. Repeat this process until there is no further change in the screw's strength. Has all the magnetism disappeared?

MATERIALS
- a steel screw, magnetized as described on page 17
- a source of heat, such as a Bunsen burner, a gas stove, or a blow torch
- a pair of pliers

WARNING!
- Ask an adult to heat the screw.

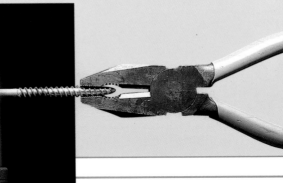

19

FIELDS

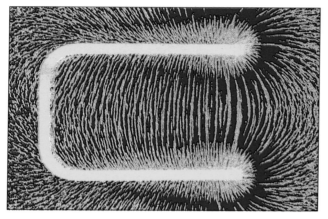

A magnet is surrounded by its magnetic field. The field is the region in which its magnetic force acts. Any magnetic material in the magnetic field will be attracted to the magnet.

This computer image of a horseshoe magnet shows how it attracts iron filings, which can be seen lined up within its magnetic field. The magnetic force is strongest near the magnet's poles, where the filings are closest together.

PLOTTING FIELDS WITH A COMPASS

1. Tape a magnet to the center of a sheet of poster board.

2. Turn the poster board over and support it with the two pieces of wood at the ends. Place the compass on top, and make pencil dots on either side of the compass to mark where the ends of its needle are pointing. Join the two dots.

3. Move the compass to another position, and repeat step **2**. Once you think you have found where a line of force is heading, try to follow it. Then look for other lines. Some lines will go from one pole to the other, but others will go off the poster board. The overall pattern should be symmetrical.

4. Repeat steps **1** to **3** with the other magnets. Try plotting the magnetic field lines between two bar magnets. Try different positions for example, north pole facing north pole, or south facing south.

MATERIALS
- several types of strong magnets
- sheets of white poster board, 8 in. x 12 in. (20 cm x 30 cm)
- two short lengths of wood the same thickness as the thickest magnet
- a small compass
- a pencil

At every point in the field, the magnetic force has a particular strength and direction. With a bar magnet, for example, the magnetic force will be strong at a point close to one of the poles and in line with the pole. It will be directed toward the south pole, and away from the north pole. But farther away from the magnet and to one side of it, the force will be weaker and acting parallel to the side. Magnets of different shapes have fields of different shapes.

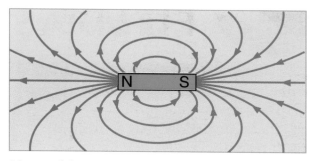

Lines of force in a bar magnet are shown as a two-dimensional slice through a three-dimensional field. The arrows indicate direction. Where the lines are closest, the field is strongest.

PLOTTING FIELDS WITH IRON FILINGS

This method keeps the iron filings from coming into contact with the magnet. Iron filings are difficult to remove from a magnet.

1. Sprinkle some iron filings evenly over a sheet of cardboard. Keep the filings away from the edges.

2. Carefully place the cardboard inside a plastic folder and seal the open sides with tape.

3. Support the cardboard inside the folder by placing the two strips of wood underneath it at either end.

4. Place a magnet underneath and tap the cardboard lightly. Look at the pattern produced by the iron filings as they arrange themselves in the magnetic field. Repeat step **3** with the other magnets.

MATERIALS
- several types of strong magnets
- sheets of white cardboard, 8 in. x 12 in. (20 cm x 30 cm)
- two short lengths of wood the same thickness as the thickest magnet
- iron filings
- a clear plastic folder, open on two sides
- masking tape

How do these patterns compare with the field lines you traced using the compass?

COMPASSES

The metal iron is found in rocks called minerals or ores. One of these minerals is called magnetite and is itself magnetic. Pieces of magnetite were used as early compasses by the Chinese nearly two thousand years ago, and in Europe from medieval times. They were known as lodestones—which means "guiding stones"—and were either suspended on a string or highly polished and placed on a smooth surface so that they were free to turn.

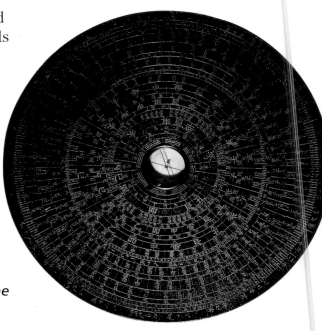

The Chinese were using compasses, like the one pictured here, centuries before European navigators began to use them.

MAKING A SUSPENDED MAGNET COMPASS

MATERIALS
- a large block of Styrofoam
- a knitting needle
- a darning needle
- a strong bar magnet
- a small test tube
- modeling clay
- a compass

1. Push the knitting needle through the Styrofoam base, so that its head is in the base. The needle should be vertical.

2. Magnetize the darning needle with the bar magnet (see page 17).

3. Attach the darning needle at its center to the base of the small test tube with a small piece of modeling clay.

4. Place the tube upside down over the point of the knitting needle. What happens? Use the compass to see in which direction the darning needle is pointing.

MAKING A FLOATING COMPASS

1. Magnetize the darning needle and tape it to a piece of cork or balsa wood.

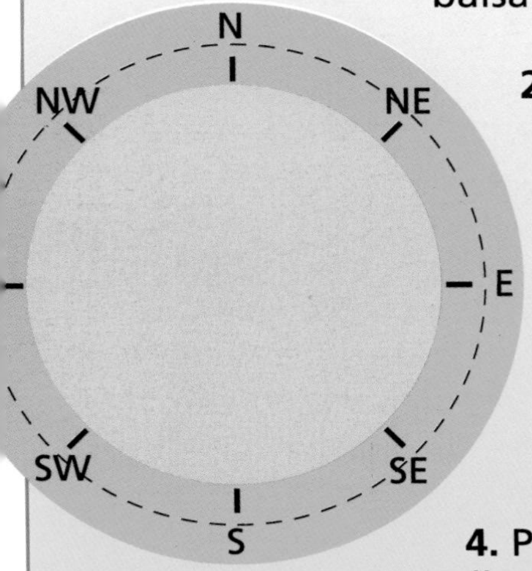

2. Cut out a ring of cardboard, as shown in the diagram, and mark on it the points of the compass.

3. Put a little water in the plate and float the needle in the center.

4. Position the marked cardboard ring around the plate with the "N" for north facing the right way.

MATERIALS
- a darning needle
- a piece of cork or balsa wood
- a strong bar magnet
- a small plate
- a piece of thin cardboard or poster board
- scissors & masking tape
- a waterproof marker

A lodestone, like the needle of a modern compass, is a magnetic material and so lines itself up with the earth's magnetic field (see page 24) to point north–south. A compass needle points to the earth's magnetic poles, which are not in quite the same place as the geographical poles. This doesn't matter if you want a rough indication of direction, but for careful navigation the difference must be allowed for. You will find the magnetic poles marked in an atlas, and "magnetic north" indicated on many maps.

Compared with most magnets, the earth's magnetic field is quite weak. A compass near a magnet will line up with its magnetic field lines. This is useful for investigating the magnet's field, but it means that compasses used for navigation must be carefully shielded from magnetic fields.

DID YOU KNOW?

Spacecraft in orbit around the earth and traveling to other planets need to navigate too. A compass is no good in space, so spacecraft orient themselves by "fixing" on one particular star.

MAGNETIC EARTH

Planet Earth has its own magnetic field, shaped like the field around a giant bar magnet. Inside the earth there are different layers. At the center is its inner core—a ball of iron and nickel 800 mi. (1,300 km) in diameter. The field is produced by the inner core's rotating slightly faster than the rest of the earth and by swirling movements in the layer outside it, the outer core.

Like any magnet, the earth has north and south magnetic poles. They lie quite close to the "geographical" poles around which the earth spins. About 30,000 years ago, the earth's magnetic field flipped over completely, with the north and south magnetic poles changing places. By studying rock formations, scientists have found that this happens every few hundred thousand years. The reason for these magnetic reversals is not yet known.

The earth's magnetic field protects us from the solar wind, which is a stream of radiation and particles constantly pouring out from the sun. The field holds back much of the solar wind, rather like a magnetic shield. The region inside this shield is called the magnetosphere. Other planets and some of their satellites have their own magnetic fields and magnetospheres. The sun and other stars also have powerful magnetic fields.

Particles in the solar wind that are captured by the earth's magnetic field sometimes light up the night sky in a colorful display called an aurora.

MODEL EARTH

1. Look in an atlas. Find a map of one hemisphere of the earth—one that shows both the north and south poles.

2. Copy the map onto a piece of cardboard. Make your map about 3 in. (8 cm) in diameter.

3. Cut out and color in your map, and mark in the geographical north and south poles.

MATERIALS
- an atlas
- two pieces of thin cardboard
- scissors
- felt-tip pens
- a ruler
- a bar magnet
- masking tape
- a small compass

4. Look in the atlas again and find where the north and south magnetic poles are. Make small marks on the back of the map to show roughly where they are.

5. On the back of the map join these two marks and tape the bar magnet so that its center runs along the line.

Rear of cardboard

Tape

Bar magnet

Pencil line

6. Make a loop of tape, sticky side out, like double-sided tape, and use it to attach your map with the magnet attached to it at the center of the second piece of cardboard.

7. Now, wherever you place the small compass, you will see the direction of the magnetic field around your model "Earth." If you wish, you can use the compass to plot the field as described on page 20.

 # MAGNETIC DOMAINS

To understand why magnets behave as they do, we need to look closely at what goes on inside them. In a ferromagnetic material, the atoms (the very smallest particles) themselves act like tiny magnets, each with a north and south pole. The atoms are grouped together in regions called domains. In a domain, all the atoms are lined up the same way, so the domain is also like a magnet, with a north and south pole. In an unmagnetized material, the domains themselves are aligned at random.

When you magnetize a piece of steel by stroking it with a magnet, the magnet pulls on the domains. If the magnet's north pole, for example, is stroked along the steel, the north poles of the domains will begin to turn around toward the direction of the stroke. Domains that are already aligned in the direction of the stroke will grow, as neighboring domains line up the same way and merge with them.

With each stroke, the aligned domains get larger. Eventually there is one very large domain in the steel, in which all the atoms face the same way, and the steel is permanently magnetized.

When a magnet is dropped or is hit with a hammer, it vibrates for a moment and this shakes up the domains. When the vibration stops, the domains settle down slightly differently, with some of them out of line with the others. The greater the jolt and the more often it happens, the weaker the magnet becomes as the arrangement of domains becomes more random.

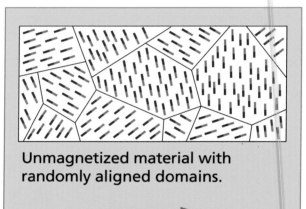

Unmagnetized material with randomly aligned domains.

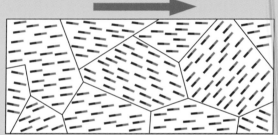

Material during the process of magnetization, showing domains merging as they gradually align in the same direction.

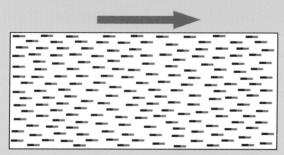

Permanently magnetized material with one large domain.

However, it is possible to magnetize a piece of steel by striking it carefully and repeatedly in the same place. This has a similar effect to stroking and helps the domains line up.

The atoms of a metal are always in motion, vibrating but staying in much the same positions. Heating a magnet causes the motion of its atoms to increase. The more the atoms move, the harder it gets for the domains to stay aligned, and above a certain temperature it becomes impossible. This temperature is called the Curie temperature.

ALIGNING DOMAINS

MATERIALS
- a small, shallow, rectangular container with a flat base
- a small quantity of long-grain rice

1. Put enough rice grains in the container just to cover the bottom.

2. Now gently tap one side of the container with your hand.

3. You will find that, here and there, small groups of rice grains will start to line up the same way. You won't be able to make the grains line up into very large "rice domains," but you will get an idea of what happens when a magnetic material is magnetized by repeatedly tapping it.

CARE AND SAFETY

With proper care, magnets will last for a long time. There are several things you can do to preserve their magnetism.

Avoid anything that you know will tend to demagnetize magnets. Always handle them carefully. Don't drop them or let them get banged around. Don't leave them in places where they might get hot. All these things will make some of the domains go out of alignment.

Domains can also slowly drift out of line even when magnets are not being used. That is why it is important to store them correctly. When a horseshoe magnet is not in use, a straight piece of iron should be placed across its poles. This is called a keeper.

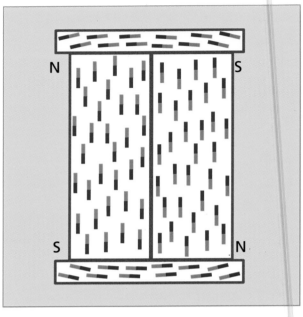

This diagram shows how to store bar magnets. The iron bars, called "keepers," at either end keep the domains aligned.

WHAT DIFFERENCE DO KEEPERS MAKE?

MATERIALS
- four identical iron nails, about 2.5 in. (6 cm) long
- a strong bar magnet
- two identical iron "keepers"
- a shoe box or box of similar size

1. Make one of the large iron nails into a permanent magnet by stroking it with the bar magnet, as you did in the activity on page 17. There is no need to make it strongly magnetized—a weakly magnetic nail will do. Write down the number of strokes.

2. Magnetize each of the other three large nails in exactly the same way. This is important if the test you are going to do is to be a fair one. Use the same number of strokes, and the same stroking motion, in the same direction.

3. Using one of the methods on pages 10–11, test the strength of your nail magnets. They should all be the same strength.

Joining the poles makes a magnetic circuit, which keeps the magnetic domains in line. Bar magnets should be kept together in pairs, north pole to south pole, preferably with an iron keeper at each end of the pair.

Keep magnets in a box that is large enough to leave space between them. Never store magnets in contact with one another (unless, like bar magnets, they are pairs of similar magnets).

You should also avoid putting magnets near certain pieces of equipment, including clocks, watches, television screens, computer monitors, and fluorescent tubes. And never put a magnet close to audio tapes, video tapes, or computer disks.

Envelopes for mailing computer disks include a printed warning about magnets.

No
No
Non
Falsch
Neen

10C - 52C
50F - 125F

Never
Nunca
Jamai:
Nie
Nooi

4. Take two of the nail magnets and place keepers across them as shown in the diagram on page 28. Put them in the shoe box at one end. Put the other two nail magnets at the other end. Lay the box to one side.

5. After an hour, measure the strength of the magnets again and make a note of your findings. Have the magnets unprotected by keepers become any weaker? Replace the magnets in the shoe box, as in step **4**.

6. Repeat the test at intervals. Judge from the results of the measurements you took in step **5** how long to wait between tests.

# MAGNETS IN ACTION

Look around, and you will find that magnets are used in many simple devices. Where something needs to be held in position but removed easily when required, a magnet is often the answer.

Magnets feature in toys and games. In train sets for younger children, the couplings between cars are sometimes magnetic. There are also toys in which a man is given different hairstyles and beards by moving iron filings around with a magnet.

In your home, look for magnets at work in the kitchen. Aside from refrigerator magnets, there may be a magnetic can opener, which holds the top after the can is opened. Some knife holders consist of several magnetic strips against which kitchen knives can be stored when they are not being used. The cupboards in the kitchen or bathroom may have magnetic door latches. Also in the bathroom, there may be a magnetic soap holder that holds the soap up so that it doesn't stay wet and slippery.

MAGNET SURVEY

1. Carry out a survey of how magnets are used in your own environment: at home, at school, and in your locality.

2. Make separate lists for where the magnets are used: kitchen, bathroom, and so on. You can also note how strong you think the magnets are in each case. Perhaps you can think of other ways to group together the magnetic devices you come across.

3. Ask some of your friends to do their own surveys. Get together and compare your findings. Think how you can combine everyone's results, and what extra things you could do. For example, how many of you have a magnetic can opener in your kitchen?

4. Ask adults to help you look for uses of magnets in garages or toolsheds. Perhaps you can extend your survey farther by finding out how magnets are used at their places of work.

Room	Magnets used for:
Kitchen	
Bathroom	
My Bedroom	
Workshop	

DID YOU KNOW?

The rather strangely shaped numbers along the bottom of a bank check are printed in magnetic ink. Banks use machines that can read these numbers and sort large numbers of checks quickly.

# MAGNETIC STORAGE

The existence of magnetic domains makes it possible to record information on what are called magnetic media. The main magnetic media are magnetic tape and magnetic disks.

Magnetic tape is used in audio-cassettes, videocassettes, and computer data cassettes. It can record sound, pictures, computer programs, and data. The tape is a long ribbon of plastic with a special coating made of either of two magnetic materials called iron oxide and chromium dioxide. You may have seen these words on tape boxes.

When the tape passes across the recording head in the audio or video tape recorder, the sound or picture signal—in the form of an electrical signal from a microphone, or video camera—is converted into magnetic signals on the tape. These signals are in the form of patterns of magnetic domains. When the tape is replayed, the playback head converts the magnetic signals back into electrical signals, which are turned into sound or pictures.

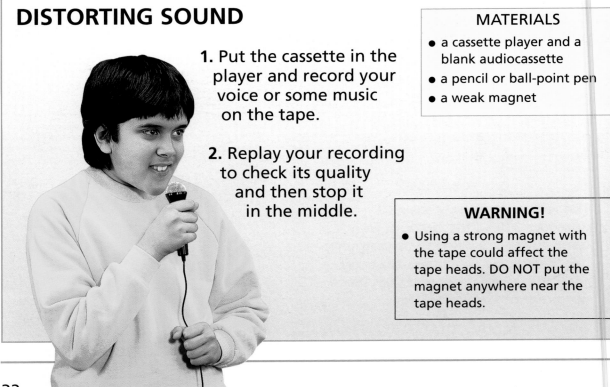

DISTORTING SOUND

1. Put the cassette in the player and record your voice or some music on the tape.

2. Replay your recording to check its quality and then stop it in the middle.

MATERIALS

- a cassette player and a blank audiocassette
- a pencil or ball-point pen
- a weak magnet

WARNING!

- Using a strong magnet with the tape could affect the tape heads. DO NOT put the magnet anywhere near the tape heads.

You should always avoid putting magnets near disks and tapes. This is because the magnets can disturb the arrangement of magnetic domains, which will interfere with the stored signal. You should also avoid placing tapes and disks on television sets and computer monitors since these generate a magnetic field when switched on or off.

Magnetic disks used in computers work in a similar way, by recording signals on a magnetic coating on the disk that can be read by a computer's disk drive. A floppy disk is a coated flexible disk housed in a plastic case that can be inserted in the computer when required. A hard disk is similar, but rigid, and housed inside the computer.

3. Now remove the cassette and stroke the exposed section of tape with the magnet.

4. Rewind it by using the pencil or pen (six-sided ones work best).

5. Replace the cassette, and replay the tape. How does the cassette sound different?

6. Redo the recording on the same section of tape.

7. Play back the new recording. How does it sound? What do you think happened to the domains on the tape when the recordings were made and when the tape was "wiped" with the magnet?

ELECTROMAGNETISM

Magnets are not the only things that attract objects with a magnetic force. An electric current passing through a wire sets up a magnetic field around the wire. The wire does not have to be a magnetic material—it just has to conduct electricity. The field lines around the wire run parallel to it.

If a wire is wound into a loop, the magnetic field lines bend around the wire; they would look something like a ring doughnut if you could see them. If the wire is looped many times to make a coil, like a spiral spring, and a current is passed through it, a stronger magnetic field is generated. This is because the field lines are concentrated together. The result is called a solenoid. The magnetic field of a solenoid has its own north and south poles. One way to magnetize an object is to place it inside a solenoid.

FIELD AROUND A WIRE

1. Push the nail through the center of the cardboard. Prop the cardboard on the four blocks.

2. Using two crocodile clips, make a circuit by connecting a length of wire to one end of the nail and a battery terminal. Connect a second length to the other battery terminal and to the switch. The third length of wire should connect the switch to the other end of the nail.

3. With the switch on, investigate the field around the third wire by moving the compass around on the cardboard.

4. With the switch off, sprinkle some iron filings around the wire.

5. Switch on again. What do you notice has happened to the filings?

MATERIALS

- a 6-volt battery
- a switch
- four crocodile clips
- three lengths of plastic-coated wire & wire stripper
- a long iron nail
- a piece of cardboard, 4 in. x 4 in. (10 cm x 10 cm)
- a small compass
- iron filings
- four wooden blocks as props

WARNING!

- Never try to wire up any of the circuits you make to house currents.

Just as electricity makes magnetism, you can create an electric current with a magnet. When a magnet is moved through a coil of wire it makes a current pass through the coil.

Electromagnetism is the name for magnetism produced by electricity. It is also the name for any effect in which electricity and magnetism are linked together.

FIELD AROUND A SOLENOID

1. Make a coil of wire by winding about 24 in. (60 cm) of wire around a piece of poster board wrapped around the broom handle. Leave about 4 in. (10 cm) of straight wire at either end. Now remove the poster board and coiled wire.

2. Connect one end of the the wire coil to the switch and the other end to the battery. Use a short length of wire to connect the switch to the battery. With the switch on, investigate the field around your solenoid by moving the small compass around it and, if the compass is small enough, inside it.

3. Sprinkle the iron filings on the small piece of poster board and carefully place it inside the plastic folder. Tape around the two open sides of the folder. Now place the sealed folder over the solenoid. What does the resulting pattern remind you of?

MATERIALS
- a broom handle
- a 6-volt battery
- a switch
- plastic-coated wire & wire stripper
- iron filings
- a piece of cardboard, 8 in. x 12 in. (20 cm x 30 cm)
- a small piece of poster board
- a plastic folder open on two sides
- masking tape
- a small compass

ELECTROMAGNETS

An electromagnet is simply a solenoid with a length of magnetic material inside it. In other words, it is a current-carrying wire coiled around a metal rod. The metal rod is called the core. Electromagnets are more powerful than ordinary magnets, and their magnetism can be switched on and off as required. They are temporary magnets. Most magnetic materials would, if used for the core, still be slightly magnetic when the current is switched off. (This is called residual magnetism.)

Cores are usually made from either a special magnetic steel or a type of iron called soft iron. Soft iron contains much less carbon than other varieties of iron and has very low residual magnetism. Sometimes a little copper is added to the iron to make the residual magnetism even lower. The strength of electromagnets, and the fact that they can be switched on and off, means that they are much more widely used than ordinary magnets. Some uses of electromagnets are described on the pages that follow.

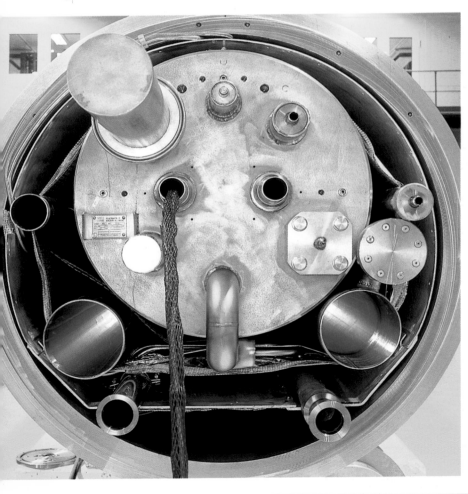

Magnet for the Large Hadron Collider (LHC). The huge LHC is the new accelerator for CERN, the European particle physics laboratory at Geneva, Switzerland.

> ### DID YOU KNOW?
> **The electromagnet with a soft-iron core was invented in 1825 by William Sturgeon, an ex-soldier. Within a few years, Gerard Moll and Joseph Henry had made electromagnets that could lift objects weighing almost a ton.**

MAKING ELECTROMAGNETS

1. Make an electromagnet by winding some plastic-coated wire around an iron nail. The length of wire you need will depend on the length of the nail. Push the coils tightly together and allow enough wire at each end for connections.

2. Complete the circuit by using the crocodile clips to connect the electromagnet to the battery and switch.

3. Switch on and test the electromagnet's strength by seeing how many paper clips it will pick up.

4. Repeat steps **1** to **3** with a steel screw of the same length. Make sure you coil the wire the same number of turns as you did for the nail. How do the results compare?

5. Think about how you might make the electromagnet stronger. Remember: for each new test to be fair—that is, for it to give results that can be exactly compared with results from other tests—if you change one variable you must keep all other variables the same. Here are some of the variables you could change: length of core, thickness of core (wrap the wire around two or more nails for a thicker core), number of turns, current (not more than two 6-volt batteries). Can you think of any others? Try to predict what will happen in each case before you do the test.

6. Collect all your results together. How would you present them?

MATERIALS

- iron nails and bolts of different lengths, over 2 in. (5 cm)
- steel screws of different lengths, over 2 in. (5 cm)
- plastic-coated wire & wire stripper
- two crocodile clips
- a 6-volt battery
- a switch
- steel paper clips

WARNING!

- Even these simple electromagnets will drain batteries quickly. For each test, switch on just beforehand and switch off as soon as you have your result.

A BURGLAR ALARM

There are probably more electromagnets than ordinary magnets in your home, although they are usually hidden inside pieces of equipment. Some houses and apartments are equipped with burglar alarms that make use of electromagnets. The burglar alarm in this project works like some real ones. When a door is opened, a circuit is broken. An electromagnet then releases a switch that completes a second circuit and sounds the alarm.

1. Cut two 6-in. (15-cm) squares of aluminum foil and fold them until they measure about 2 in. x .75 in. (5 cm x 2 cm). These will be the electrical contacts.

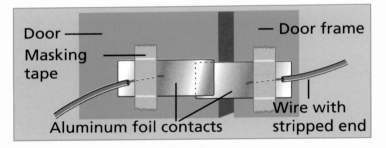

Door — Door frame
Masking tape
Aluminum foil contacts
Wire with stripped end

2. Tape the stripped end of a 20-in. (50-cm) length of wire to one of the contacts. Now tape it near the base of a door frame.

3. Tape the other contact and a similar length of wire to the door. The door-frame contact should be held between the door contact and the door. Make sure that the two contacts touch.

4. Make an electromagnet by winding another length of wire around the iron nail. Join one end of the electromagnet coil to the other end of the wire attached to the door-frame contact.

5. Clip the end of the wire attached to the door contact to a battery and switch, making sure the switch is in the off position. Complete the first circuit by joining the switch to the other end of the electromagnet coil.

6. Nail one of the 6-in. (15-cm) lengths of wood to the baseboard and the other piece to the top of the upright.

7. To start the second circuit, join one end of a short length of wire to the thumbtack. Attach the wire to the buzzer. Join the buzzer to the other battery and switch (again, with the switch off) and wire the switch to the paper clip. Position the paper clip so that the end not attached to the wire lies on the thumbtack. Tape the wire joined to it to the base.

8. Now tape the electromagnet to the frame and position it so that its end is just above the unconnected end of the paper clip. Switch on the first circuit. The electromagnet will lift the paper clip clear of the thumbtack.

9. Switch on the second circuit. Your burglar alarm is now set. When the door is opened, the foil contacts will part and the first circuit will be broken. The electromagnet will release the paper clip, which will drop onto the thumbtack and complete the second circuit. The buzzer will go off.

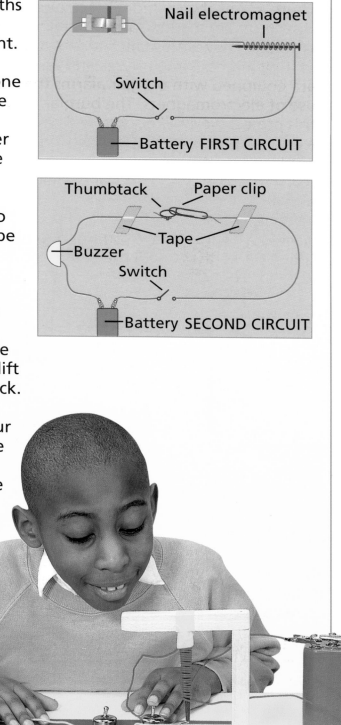

Nail electromagnet

Switch

Battery FIRST CIRCUIT

Thumbtack   Paper clip

Tape

Buzzer

Switch

Battery SECOND CIRCUIT

TRANSFORMERS

A wire with a current flowing through it has a magnetic field around it. Also, a current can be made to flow through a wire when a magnet is moved past it. If you put these two things together, you have a very useful device called a transformer.

A transformer is basically an electromagnet with two separate coils of wire wrapped around the same core, called the former. The first coil is connected to the primary circuit, and the second coil to the secondary circuit. When the current in the primary circuit is switched on, a magnetic field spreads through the former in a fraction of a second, like a balloon inflating very quickly.

The second coil "thinks" a magnet has moved through it very quickly, and a current flows in the secondary circuit. But as soon as the magnetic field has stopped growing, the current vanishes. The opposite happens when the current in the primary circuit is switched off. The magnetic field shrinks quickly to nothing, and a current briefly flows in the secondary circuit, but in the opposite direction.

The blue box in this racing car set is a transformer. Its job is to reduce the house current supply to a lower voltage.

An alternating current in the primary circuit will reverse direction many times a second. The magnetic field passing through the second coil will then change constantly, so an alternating current will flow through the secondary circuit for as long as the first current is on.

What use is this? We often need to change a low voltage into a high one, or vice versa. A transformer that has more coils in its secondary, "output," circuit than in its primary, "input," circuit will have a higher output voltage—it is called a step-up transformer. A step-down transformer works the other way around.

Large step-up transformers are used at power stations to boost the voltage to nearly half a million volts before electric power is transmitted around the country. Step-down transformers near our homes bring this down to house current voltage (125 volts). Many small electrical domestic appliances and games operate at a low voltage and use step-down transformers to reduce the house current to just a few volts.

INVESTIGATING TRANSFORMERS

1. Make a primary circuit of an electromagnet by coiling the wire 20 turns around one end of the knitting needle. Connect this to the switch and battery.

2. Make the secondary circuit by winding 10 turns of wire around the other end of the knitting needle. Coil the wire 10 times around a piece of poster board wrapped around the broom handle. Remove the poster board and coil from the broom handle and attach the coil to the secondary circuit.

3. Switch on and watch the compass needle when you place it in the coil. What is happening?

4. Repeat the test, each time increasing the number of turns in the primary circuit. How does the compass respond each time?

# ELECTRIC MOTORS

You have seen that when a magnet moves through a coil, an electric current flows in the coil. A current would also flow if you moved the coil around the magnet, and this is what makes an electric motor work. In the simplest form of electric motor, a coil of wire is free to spin between the poles of a magnet. Current from a battery passes through the coil. The wires from the battery are attached to the coil by wires that press against a commutator, a metal ring in two halves, at the end of the coil.

When the current flows, a magnetic field is induced in the coil. The coil flips around so that the north pole of the field points to the south pole of the magnet. But because the wires from the battery are now pressing against the opposite halves of the commutator, the magnetic field in the coil changes direction, and the coil flips around again. The field then reverses again, and the coil keeps on spinning. A small basic motor like this can power simple devices like a handheld fan.

MAKING A SIMPLE ELECTRIC MOTOR

1. Push the two corks onto the knitting needle. The needle should pass through their centers. Move the corks to the middle of the needle, with about .5 in. (1 cm) between them.

2. Wind some insulated copper wire around the large cork, about 10 turns, and tape the two ends to the small cork. Cut off any surplus wire.

3. Hammer the nails into the wooden base in two pairs, to make X-shaped supports for the knitting needle. Make sure the needle spins freely.

4. Tape the two magnets to the wooden blocks on either side of the large cork, with opposite poles facing each other. They must be at the same height as the needle. Be sure they are at the right height before you tape them in position.

MATERIALS

- a wooden base, 8 in. x 12 in. (20 cm x 30 cm), and .75 in. (2 cm) thick
- two small blocks of wood
- four strong thin nails
- a knitting needle
- two corks, one large and one small
- plastic-coated wire
- thin, insulated copper wire
- two magnets with their poles on their flat surfaces (face polarized)
- a 6-volt battery
- a switch
- masking tape
- hammer & wire stripper
- thumbtacks

This arrangement can work in reverse: if the coil is spun at a steady rate, a current will be generated in it. This is more or less how a dynamo works. The difference is that here the magnet is on the inside and the coil (actually an electromagnet, since it is wrapped around an iron core) is on the outside. It is the magnet spinning around that generates the electricity. Power stations use what are in effect giant dynamos to generate electricity.

An electric bus being recharged after a trip around a city center. The driver is plugging the bus directly into the city's electricity supply.

5. Strip the coating from the ends of two short lengths of plastic-coated wire. Connect the battery and switch as in the diagram.

6. Using drawing pins, fix the bare ends of the wire so that they press against the copper wire on the small cork.

Nails · Knitting needle · Large cork · Magnets · Copper wire · Small cork · Nails · Battery · Switch · Plastic-coated wire

7. Switch on, and your motor should start to turn. You may have to experiment with the positions of the magnets.

WARNING!
• Ask an adult to pierce the corks and to strip the coating from the ends of the wire. Also ask the adult to hammer in the nails for you.

 # MAGNETS AT WORK

Wherever you look in the modern world—in industry, commerce, transportation, communications, medicine, entertainment—you will find electromagnets. Their use in motors and transformers means that there are very few machines or pieces of electrical equipment in which they do not play a role. There's room for just a few examples here.

In scrapyards, all sorts of discarded objects, metal and nonmetal, arrive together and are dumped in great heaps. A crane with a powerful electromagnet in place of a hook or "grab" is used to lift out the iron and steel scrap (called "ferrous" scrap) to separate it from the nonferrous materials. Iron and steel recovered in this way and recycled in steel plants is used for making new steel products.

Many assembly lines in factories, in particular those producing automobiles, are now operated mostly by industrial robots. They are not like the metal men from science fiction, but they do have "arms," which they use to move parts such as metal body panels into position. The "hands" are often electromagnets, which switch on to pick up, and switch off to put down.

This is a maglev train (short for "magnetic levitation"). Powerful magnetic fields in the train and the track repel each other, lifting the train clear of the track.

If you've flown on an airplane, you know that before you board your flight you have to pass through a large metal detector at the airport. This is like a large archway, inside which are powerful electromagnets. The idea is to detect weapons being carried by potential hijackers, but of course it will detect anything else made of metal. If you forget to take all your coins out of your pocket before you pass through, you will set off the alarm.

Anyone unfortunate enough to get a fragment of metal in an eye could meet a medical electromagnet at the hospital. Once a surgeon has carefully positioned the instrument containing the magnet over the metal fragment, it is switched on and pulls the fragment clear.

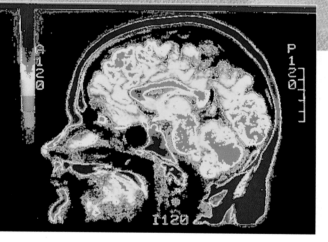

Top: A radiology technician prepares a patient for a magnetic resonance imaging (MRI) brain scan. The subject's head is surrounded by the large coils of the scanner's magnet; the smaller device above the subject's head is a radio frequency receiver. MRI scanning uses radio waves and a magnetic field to produce images of cross-sectional "slices" through the body.

Inset: An MRI scan of the side view of a male human head containing a healthy brain.

GLOSSARY

Attraction The "pull" of a magnet, or the force between a north and south pole.

Demagnetization The process of making a magnet lose some or all of its magnetism—the opposite of magnetization.

Domain A tiny region that is magnetized in a particular direction inside a magnetic material.

Electromagnet A solenoid with a core of magnetic material inside it.

Electromagnetism Magnetism produced by electricity.

Ferromagnetic material A material that can be made permanently magnetic.

Keeper A straight piece of iron placed across the poles of a magnet not in use.

Lodestone A piece of magnetite used as a compass.

Magnet A solid object with the power to attract iron or other metals.

Magnetic field The region within which a magnet's magnetic force acts.

Magnetic materials Substances that a magnet will attract.

Magnetic media The term for all types of recording tape and computer disks with magnetic coatings on which information is recorded.

Magnetic shield A barrier made from a magnetic material, which keeps a magnetic field out or in.

Magnetism The force that attracts objects to a magnet.

Magnetite A magnetic mineral (rock) containing iron.

Magnetization or **magnetic induction** The process of turning an object made of a magnetic material into a magnet.

Permanent magnet A magnet that stays magnetized permanently (or at least for a long time).

Pole Either one of the ends of a magnet, through which it exerts the greatest force.

Repulsion The force that pushes two like poles (both north or both south) away from each other.

Residual magnetism The small amount of magnetism left in an electromagnet when the current is switched off.

Soft iron Iron with very little carbon in it, used for the cores of electromagnets.

Solenoid A coil of wire through which a current is passed to create a magnetic field.

Temporary magnet A magnet that stays magnetized for only a short time.

Transformer An electromagnetic device for changing a low voltage into a high one, or vice versa.

BOOKS TO READ

Friedhoffer, Robert. *Magnetism and Electricity.* Danbury, CT: Franklin Watts, 1992.

Gardner, Robert. *Electricity and Magnetism.* (Yesterday's Science, Today's Technology.) New York: 21st Century Books, 1994.

———. *Science Projects About Electricity and Magnetism.* Springfield, NJ: Enslow Publishers, 1994.

Kerrod, Robin. *Electricity and Magnetism.* (Let's Investigate Science.) Tarrytown, NY: Marshall Cavendish, 1994.

Wong, Ovid K. *Experiments with Electricity and Magnetism.* (Venture.) Danbury, CT: Franklin Watts, 1993.

ANSWERS TO QUESTIONS

Answers to questions posed in the projects.

Page 7 Some of your metal objects may be non-magnetic. Most kitchen foil, for example, is made of aluminum, which is a nonmagnetic material.

Pages 8–9 The suspended magnet will move toward the one you are holding when unlike poles are facing each other, and away from it when like poles are facing each other. The second bar magnet "floats" above the first one (without the toothpicks, it would not stay in place).

Pages 10–11 Both methods should give the same results.

Pages 12–13 In general, magnetic force penetrates thin or low-density materials more easily than thick or dense ones. A magnet works under water but less well than in air. One requirement for a fair test would be that samples of different materials should all be of equal thickness.

Page 15 The lid of a can is usually made of steel and will act as a magnetic shield. Other materials, provided they are not too thick, will not act as shields because the magnetic force will penetrate them.

Pages 16–17 A temporary magnet always loses its magnetism when the inducing magnet is taken away. The iron nail should make a stronger temporary or permanent magnet. Stroking the nail with two magnets will magnetize it more quickly.

Pages 18–19 All three methods will sooner or later cause complete demagnetization. You will find that more hammer blows than heating cycles are needed to demagnetize a screw.

Pages 20–21 The field you plot for a bar magnet should look something like the diagram on page 21. If you have been able to draw them well enough, the field lines between like poles and between unlike poles of two bar magnets might suggest to you why there is repulsion and attraction. The patterns you get with the filings should be roughly the same as the plotted fields.

Page 22 The test-tube pivots on the point of the knitting needle, and the darning needle aligns itself north–south.

Pages 28–29 You should find that the nail magnets protected by keepers retain their magnetism for longer.

Pages 32–33 The sound on the section of tape "wiped" by the magnet will be distorted and may even be unrecognizable as your voice or as music. After re-recording, the sound should be as it was originally. Wiping the tape partly destroyed the pattern of domains in which the sound signal was stored. Re-recording restored the pattern.

Pages 34–35 The compass will show that the field lines around the wire are circles centered on the wire. The iron filings will arrange themselves to follow this pattern. The field lines in the solenoid all pass through the inside in the same direction and loop around the outside and back in again. The pattern of filings should be similar to what you found for the field around a bar magnet.

Page 37 An iron nail makes a better electromagnet core than a steel screw does. A thicker core (more nails), more turns, and a higher current (two batteries) will all make the electromagnet stronger.

Page 41 When the current is first switched on, the compass needle flickers once, as the magnetic field spreads out, then settles back when the field is steady. With each increase of the number of turns in the primary circuit, the flicker of the needle will be greater.

INDEX